The Corporate Bawarchi

(The Forgotten '*Unsung Hero*' of Successful Corporates)

Usha Saroj

BEEJA
HOUSE

ISBN : 978-93-93635-58-7 (Paperback)

Published by: Beeja House

First Printing Edition 2022

Author Email: usharanee.panda@gmail.com & sarroj.patro@gmail.com

Series Editors: Lopamudra Patro & Vidipta Patro

Dedication

To the Invisible "Supreme Power"

Who has Motivated the Authors

to Conceptualize and Write this Book,

for the Betterment of the Society

Disclaimer

All characters and incidents portrayed and the names (and, situations) used in this book are fictitious and any resemblance to reality is purely co-incidental. Any similarity or resemblance to the name, character or history of any person (living or dead), is entitely and purely co-incidental and unintentional. The script of the book, all charcaters, locations, and incidents mentioned are entirely fictionalized. Neither the content of this book, nor the writers (and, series editors), characters associated with this book intend to malign, defame, offend or hurt to any human being (living or dead), any profession, corporates, organizations, places, regions, countries. This book has been written for the purpose of literary contributions. The writers, editors associated with this book are all law-abiding citizens and have not contributed to this book to incite any disorder or lawlessness.

Contents

Introduction

'Bawarchi' is derived from Hindi literature, which means 'Chef' or 'Cook.' The role of a Bawarchi is immense for the reputation of a Hotel, Restaurant, and festive occasions. In olden times, we have heard stories about how the Kings and Emperors like the great Akbar and the wise Vikramaditya (or, the 2nd Chandra Gupta of the Gupta dynasty) had employed very efficient cooks in their royal kitchens, during their empire periods. Yet, anyone hardly knows about the names of these cooks. Many of us have also heard stories about how the great cooks made very delicious food for the entire community, during a festive occasion and how people used to flock to eat those tasty foods. The success of a festive occasion depended on the success of the food-making capability of the talented Bawarchi. In most cases, no one bothers about him while consuming the food and he often remains an 'UNSUNG' hero. He prepares tasty food tirelessly throughout his life for others. He makes his food out of raw vegetables, masala/spices, other food items, etc. He uses all his experience, and fondness for the service of food offering to others. Only in recent times, thanks to the growth of social media, we are getting to know about a few popular Indian and International chefs and cooks who have made their presence felt. However, their names are very limited.

Through this book, the 'authors-duo' tries to correlate the heart-touching story of a dedicated engineer/ employee throughout his work-life at different organisations to that of the sincere Bawarchi's work, silently, in the background. The main hero of this story, named Sarvesh, has rendered selfless service more than was expected of him in any of his organisations and yet he remains the 'unsung' hero of the corporate field. He moves from one place to another in search of his real master who would reward him for his dedication at work. Have you seen such a Real Master who would recognise and reward Sarvesh for his work? If so, please suggest and drop us an email and you could be the next person to meet Sarvesh in reality. He would share some tips about corporate life for your benefit, all at no cost. This type of character is relevant in the modern-day workplace scenarios and it's time to recognise his hard work or else there shall be a time when the organisations would struggle for relevance in their respective domain, in the absence of such people.

This book is for anyone who wants to elevate their career and life, by doing the right things. It attempts to highlight the areas of work-life where one needs to be careful about and to avoid a trap. Be it a student, an employee, a fresh college graduate, an industry veteran, a teacher, a scientist, an engineer, a doctor, etc. This book is for everyone to get enlightened about how to lead a balanced life at work and at home.

The Authors thank their readers with the highest level of gratitude who take the contents of this book with utmost sincerity. Positive and constructive feedback and comments about this book are most welcome which would help the authors to deliver even better writings, in their future endeavors.

Chapter-1

A Tale of Two Interviews

It was Sarvesh's 20th Wedding Anniversary night on June 7, 2020. He was doing his best to come to terms with what had occurred over the last year while working 24 hours a day, seven days a week, for one of the new start-up companies. It had negatively impacted his health owing to overwork and various other problems. He had only recently returned from the hospital in April of that year. He and his wife were attempting to forget the ordeals that had befallen him, her and their children. He experienced a near-death experience as the family's primary breadwinner, and he thanked God for his survival and ability to emerge strong from that catastrophe.

As they say, there is a silver lining to every storm, and there is a ray of hope after Pandora's box released the 'HOPE-agent' to offer new life to people like him and his wife. Of course, with this month being their month of joy since they met 20 years ago, he was stumped about what gift he could give his wife. He had nothing unique to offer except the consolation his wife had given him that one day God would grant them the deserving life they intended to be living. Surprisingly, on the wedding anniversary day, her words of optimism came true! Sarvesh received a call from Jay, an HR representative from a large MNC company (Whizwin Corp). He stated, "Sarvesh, you applied for a position over a month ago, and your profile has been short-listed, out of many candidates, and our team of technical specialists from abroad wants to speak with you." Sarvesh had nearly forgotten that he had applied for this position a month before going to the hospital for treatment. He had filled the application for that job, expecting it might or might not materialize. However, God may have set up this channel for him, perfectly timed now that he had returned from the hospital, after a month of treatment and post-treatment recovery.

While speaking with Jay, all of the previous month's events flashed through his mind. Also, because the job was in another city, he was unsure whether he would be able to move there, even if he did get it. However, he put all of his concerns to rest when he replied, "Sure, I'm available for the discussions." Jay also informed him that if he were successful in each passing round, he would face several more rounds of interviews. He was nervous from within due to the sheer number of interviews, but he managed to control his emotions and agreed to attend the interviews, hoping to give his best effort. Before they finished talking, the HR representative told him he would schedule those interviews in the Google meeting calendar over the next few weeks. Sarvesh looked at his wife after putting down his phone, unsure whether he could sustain so many rounds of interviews at this stage of his long career. On the other hand, his wife Shalini was full of confidence in his capabilities and talent and in her God, in whom she had complete faith.

Shalini and Sarvesh were head over heels in love from the moment they first saw each other, and their love only got more robust with each passing year. Anyway, they went to bed that night after eating some light supper. Sarvesh used to hum good old Hindi songs having a theme before going to sleep. That night, he performed some Hindi songs to help her forget about the previous negative things that had transpired with him and make their 20th wedding anniversary a happy occasion. Overall, it was a pleasant evening with Shalini, who was relieved to see her husband again, fit and well, following his successful treatment. Both thanked God, and their 20th wedding anniversary was a success.

The HR representative contacted the next day and provided the meeting calendar for Day-one, the first round of interviews. Marc H was the name of the individual who conducted the Day-one interview. He was a lively and energetic individual with a very appealing manly demeanour. With whomever he spoke, he sounded like he was driving a command. He was, nevertheless, entirely professional in allowing the other individual with whom he interacted sufficient opportunity. He knew when to command, when to start and stop, and even when to let others speak for themselves. He was a well-balanced professional. Sarvesh sensed Marc's fiery demeanour within the first five minutes. Marc loved early morning interviews in the India time zone, as it was the conclusion of a long day for him. As a result, he appeared to have flawlessly timed the interview within the one-hour time limit.

"Sarvesh Kumar, from your long career of twenty-plus years, I see that you have lasted the longest seven years in your first firm, Department of Wireless and Informatics (DWI), and then you could not stay anywhere else that long," Marc began by asking him. So, what were some of the positive aspects of your first position? "Could you elaborate?" Sarvesh was a little apprehensive when he heard this question because he was expecting a technical question, initially. But, the first one was more of a behavioral type. Regardless, he rapidly regained self-awareness and attempted to navigate his past. He described the utter exhilaration of landing his first job after graduating with an engineering degree in the year 2000. Sarvesh expressed his joy at landing his first job, as a Research Scientist, in India's top Research and Development (R&D) organization, DWI. He was always the best student in his college class and was well ahead of his peers. This prestigious and well-paying job was located in the silicon valley of India, Bangalore. As a result, it was a proud occasion for him, his parents, and his extended family. With this position, his parents, and four brothers were ecstatic, including his elder sister's family. They immediately began to spread the word to all of their known circles across their home state and beyond.

Sarvesh was the third child of his parents. His elder brother Pramod was five years senior to him. His elder brother and elder sister were both twins. While Sarvesh was as humble as ever with his accomplishment, his siblings were not. With this event, the family members regained their social status after many years of living in an unknown and undesirable social status. Of course, at the time, Sarvesh's success seemed to have a lot of prestige for his family members. Hence, they didn't waste any opportunity to get their attention by highlighting Sarvesh's name and success. It appeared to be their achievement, but they were trying to get the most out of it. Sarvesh was unaware of what was happening because he had complete trust in his extended family members. Getting an R&D job in Bangalore was a dream for many, but it had already come true for Sarvesh, and his family members were already encashing it. They appeared to be eager to gain the attention of their friends and family.

Sarvesh's father ran a business, but it was on the verge of bankruptcy by the time this job offer arrived. As a result, his father emotionally forced him to look for work after finishing his bachelor's degree in college. Sarvesh had always attended a government school and college, never burdening his family, and was always striving for a better life for them. Sarvesh's father was born in North India but has lived with his family in West Bengal for many years. Sarvesh used to offer tuition to school and college students during his studies, and with that money, he used to buy books, pay school and college fees, and so on. So, even though he had the opportunity and talent to pursue higher education, he had to put his desires and aspirations on hold. Instead, he rejoiced in sacrificing his dreams to fulfil his father's wish, and to support the family's financial situation since his elder brother was helpless and unable to support the family any longer.

Sarvesh had already given up his first significant ambition: to become a qualified professor in a prestigious university abroad after receiving a PhD (i.e., doctorate degree) from an elite institute. Instead, he had to choose the path of getting this job which he had just achieved. In any case, he had to change his career path and instead chose to pursue a scientific engineering career in an R&D organization because his family did not support his first wish of furthering his higher education, he had to pursue a career in which he could at least indirectly contribute to the growth of his country. Of course, he had the opportunity to pursue a career in Software Engineering with reputable Indian MNC companies. Still, he never chose that path because he had a strong research interest. As he continued his scientific work, he got inspired by Dr APJ Abdul Kalam, a prominent personality and an inspirational figure in the Indian scientific community. He had some job offers from Central Government research labs, but he had to decline them because they came after his job offer from DWI. Of course, another reason was for those other government jobs; he was supposed to live in a government hostel for the first few years. In that case, he could not have kept his parents and brothers with him at his future Bangalore residence. While working as a DWI scientific officer, he had the good fortune of living in an independent house with his parents and brothers in Bangalore. This was also one of the main reasons he chose DWI over other government jobs.

It was also the year 2000 when a devastating Natural Calamity of Flood hit his home state of West Bengal. During this time, his father's house was damaged, and he had no proper work or job for a good living. So it appeared as if God had given him this job at the perfect time. This job selection procedure included an All India level written test, followed by an interview for those who passed the test. He was the most talented, and due to his hard work and talent, he was one of the deserving sixty-three candidates who were selected for DWI that year across Pan-India. There were a total of twenty thousand students who had appeared for the DWI written test that year.

While Sarvesh was about to embark on his new career path, he thought it would be appropriate to consult with his college professors, as he felt the need to take their advice before embarking on this path. His professors thought he'd go into academia because of his brilliance in that field. But, because he was already on a different track, some of them thought he could try to persuade his parents to let him prioritize academics over a job. However, his college Department Head Prof CK Chatterjee Sir advised him not to be selfish and to listen to his parents and put their interests ahead of his own. He also explained how, despite being a first-generation IITian (i.e., those who study at the Indian Institute of

Technology), he sacrificed his career and stayed in his home state in the post-independence era. He told Sarvesh that he was the youngest son of his parents and that his mother wanted him to stay close to her until she died, so he stayed. Prof Chatterjee also attempted to persuade him that the DWI job is very lucrative. He strongly advised Sarvesh to take only the DWI route. The professor also told him how that organization had helped the Indian scientific and engineering landscape by reaching out to the masses, meeting their needs, and improving their quality of life through various research innovations. So, as a result of this discussion, Sarvesh became motivated and felt obligated to respect his father's wishes and refused to listen to anyone else.

Sarvesh's new organisation had sent him a luxurious second Class AC (i.e., Air Conditioned) train fare for him and his family while he was preparing to travel to Bangalore by train. When his family was struggling those days to travel in a Normal Sleeper berth, this AC ticket for the entire family was a completely different experience for them. Everyone was very excited about this, and they were also rejoicing and looking forward to their train ride. Sarvesh's elder brother was also on the passenger list for this trip. So far, his elder brother, Pramod, had been assisting his father in his business, and he was a college dropout who had never received good grades in college and had even failed. The only time he received reasonably average grades was in his high school days. Sarvesh was tall and innocent, but his elder brother was short and shrewd. He had already tried several tricks in the family business, but they had failed. Instead, the quick tricks had backfired, and the business had declined even further on the path to collapse.

It is noteworthy to mention that Sarvesh maintained his focus on his studies and grades throughout the period of difficult financial circumstances. During his college days, he went without proper food for days and weeks, but he maintained a balance and stability of mind and body and did not reveal his hardships to anyone. In these matters, he was a very private person. He had a strong personality and gentleness, but he also had a flexible attitude towards people and friends. He was the focal point for his batch mates during college, and they relied on him for assistance with studies and practical lab sessions. He had always genuinely helped those around him. Sarvesh's excellent academics and command of engineering subjects had, in some ways, impressed the DWI selection team. This was the key reason this DWI job had come about.

The family business was nearing its end, and the flood had broken his family's backbone. So his brother was also at a loss for what to do next in his life. This DWI job was a ray of hope at this point, and it was like fresh oxygen in Sarvesh's family and living. Pramod wanted to start over in Bangalore. After arriving in Bangalore, he began his studies with Sarvesh's unconditional financial and overall sponsorship, enrolling in an IT (i.e., Information Technology) college in Bangalore.

Later on, this education helped Pramod immensely. He is now a well-established and happy man in his life, living in one of the Scandinavian countries with his family and children. Returning to Sarvesh's episode, he thanked God once more for this job opportunity to save and serve his family when they were in desperate need.

On a beautiful day, everyone began their trip to Bangalore. There was an aura of exhilaration. His father, Umakant, was ecstatic and expressed his joy to nearly everyone on the train for the next twenty-four hours of their trip. However, Pramod and the mother were not comfortable with Umakant's frankness. They were the type of individuals that constantly attempted to keep good things and joys to themselves. Umakant was different and was more extroverted. This trait of his had caused him nothing but trouble throughout his life. He was fed up with his business and sorely needed this change in his life, and he was significantly happier than Sarvesh. Umakant had already resolved to retire early from his business. He intended to settle down for the remainder of his life. He had not even come close to the average retirement age. Since he was an avid fan of Indian movies and gramophone records, he began to devote most of his time to these pursuits, as soon as this job offer materialized.

During this train ride, Umakant would converse with food and tea vendors who sold their goods to passengers. He liked to tell people that DWI had invited his son to serve the country and accomplish crucial initiatives based on future technologies. The train passengers did not comprehend much. Still, they respected that despite originating from a meagre family, Sarvesh had landed an excellent R&D position, a rare accomplishment in those times. This train ride was so memorable that it still feels like a dream. Most people today cannot appreciate life's valuable moments, yet in the past, every small and large event greatly enriched people's lives. Similarly, Sarvesh's family was also experiencing delight and success.

After the family arrived in Bangalore, DWI reserved a guest house for two weeks until a permanent residence became available through the company's leased accommodation. The administrative department at DWI was efficient, and with their assistance, Sarvesh was assigned a magnificent, sizable three-bedroom house. This residence was leased for at least four years, and the organization intended to pay the monthly rent. This residence of fourteen hundred square feet in the city's centre was a royal treatment for this family of humble origins in those days. In light of this, Sarvesh's family appeared to be in a paradisiacal location.

Bangalore is known as the Silicon Valley in India, as it is home to all the big MNCs (i.e., Multinational Corporations), several reputable central government offices and other R&D organizations. Having such a secure and recognised position in Bangalore was much rare and prestigious for Sarvesh, in those days. In October, when his family first arrived in Bangalore, it rained nearly every evening, and it was freezing in the morning. In terms of weather, the daytime used to be exceptionally pleasant. Every morning, Sarvesh would consume a light breakfast at home before taking the office cab to work. His family gradually acclimated to Bangalore, and his new office became a vital part of his daily routine.

Chapter-2

Corporate Bawarchi's First Dish

Within the DWI organization, new engineers were referred to as recent grads (or GETs for short). The department allocation was a crucial factor for the GETs. In a sense, this determined the remainder of the new engineers' careers within the organization and their entire careers. Sarvesh was assigned to a department responsible for the most challenging R&D tasks. However, this kind of employment was extraordinarily specialized and highly regarded in countries such as the United States, the United Kingdom, etc. This position needed much attention and personal effort to study many books, periodicals, and global organizations' practical works. While his batch mates in the GET program preferred to work in other software departments, Sarvesh preferred to remain in this field. While studying engineering, he demonstrated an interest in this field. His other GET friends did not choose this field since they did not foresee significant employment opportunities in that field in India at the time. Since most GETs were in their early twenties and desired to spend their free time conversing with female batch mates and other spare time activities, they did not wish to commit time and effort for this field.

Most of the persons in Sarvesh's department were over the age of 40, and the majority were male. Initially, he devoted a substantial portion of his day to everyday work and his evenings to a great deal of work-related research at the library. His batch mates were annoyed that he chose a field that left him with little time for anything else. Eventually, he also discovered some musical pastimes, but only after completing his first significant project assignment!

There were three managers in the department, and Sarvesh was assigned to one of them during the initial term of department assignment. The first manager came from a Malayalam-speaking family, the second from a Hindi-speaking family, and the third from a Bengali-speaking family. A Bengali named Ayan Ghosh served as Sarvesh's manager. He was a tall man with a fair complexion and thick-framed glasses. Bengali heavily influenced his English and occasionally blended with Hindi terms, which sometimes sounded amusing. When he was chatting with people, he tended to stare at them through his spectacles with his huge eyes. Sarvesh, the new engineer, was getting annoyed by this. Ayan seemed to have developed a habit of examining people's facial expressions and attempting to decipher their psyche! Sarvesh has never met somebody like this before at that age. This manager was delighted to have Sarvesh join his team. In reality, he didn't have a large team with him at the moment, and Sarvesh was the only new GET who had joined him that year, with only a few technicians reporting to him.

On the day Sarvesh joined the group, there was another member who was on vacation. Praful Garg was the guy in question, and he had resigned and was serving his notice term. As a result, Ayan was excitedly anticipating the arrival of a new GET to replace Praful and, as a result, to receive the knowledge transfer from him before his departure. Sarvesh quickly got to know that Praful would be leaving the organization in days, not weeks! He understood he had almost landed in a critical period in that department. Furthermore, it became evident over time that Ayan and Praful were not on speaking terms. Praful did not impart any useful knowledge to Sarvesh. Ayan was so scared of Praful the outgoing individual that he never pressed him to hand over the items properly. It was evident that Sarvesh was already in a sticky situation, and he didn't have enough time to respond or complain to anyone about it.

Praful was on excellent terms with Ayan's boss, therefore, he was able to leave the organization without being held responsible for not completing his tasks. For obvious reasons, Ayan did not put any pressure on him either. Instead, he began motivating Sarvesh by saying, "Look, Sarvesh, this person, Praful, has not done any useful work throughout his three years in our organization, and finishing his half-completed work will not be that difficult." You can do anything if you put forth some effort, and I will assist you." Since Ayan was present, Sarvesh assumed he would advise him on how to complete Praful's unfinished work, in whatever format it was at the time. However, he gradually recognized that Ayan was only saying superficial things and that he lacked in-depth knowledge of Praful's work. No one in that department had a good understanding of what Praful had done and how he had done it. The only thing he had was a physical module, a half-complete design, and some hand-drawn sketches of Ayan to use as a reference.

Ayan had given Sarvesh a few months to learn the job. He set him a goal of finishing all of the documentation, test reports, real testing, and re-creating the complete design layout, circuit diagram, and so on. This task appeared to be similar to climbing Everest. Sarvesh was battling inside since he didn't have any details and wasn't given any support whatsoever. His batch mates were having fun at work and in life, while he devoted additional time to learning the complexities of Praful's incomplete job. As a result of all of this, he was reaching home late, almost every night. His mother used to be concerned about why he was often late. She used to tell him that he shouldn't spend so much time at work and should instead focus on his health. Neither she nor the rest of the family realized the magnitude of his situation. He knew that such superficial advice would be of no use to him. He also considered leaving that employment in a non-supportive workplace and looking for work elsewhere. However, he couldn't take any drastic decisions because he was concerned about his family's social standing. But he was breaking from the inside out.

At this juncture, he had one option: accept the challenge and then rise to the situation. He had overcome many difficulties during his studies and always triumphed. He collected strength from inside, slowly but steadily. He began spending long nights in the lab, attempting to decipher some of Praful's older designs from the office computer to see if there was any similarity with the one he had left unfinished. He also spoke with Praful's wife, Rozy Madhavan, who was still an employee in that organization but in a different department. Sarvesh requested her to assist him by setting up a meeting with Praful. Rozy is a Tamilnadu native who married Praful in a love marriage while working at DWI. Praful was from North India and had an attractive appearance and the ability to persuade anyone with his words, especially the opposing gender.

Sarvesh had already learned more about Praful as a person from the gossip of his coworkers in the department at this time. According to others, Praful had a clear and crisp plan in all he did to carry out his intentions, and he also could manipulate others to his advantage. Earlier, while Praful was away, the other coworkers used their free time to gossip about his marriage. Rozy, on the other side, was quiet, composed, and laser-focused, whereas Praful was flashy. She was attractive enough, with long hair, a round face, and dark eyes, as seen in typical south Indian young women deeply rooted in tradition. She was technically more talented than her spouse, according to most people.

While the series of events were progressing, Praful was already working in another top private Multinational company on the outskirts of Bangalore city. Sarvesh managed to take a day off work and meet Praful in the reception area of his new company, where he requested that he explain the details of his unfinished design. Praful, on the other hand, was hesitant to reveal the inner workings of his half-finished project, opting instead for a high-level overview that Ayan had already briefed him on. "Sarvesh, please invest a little more time yourself to grasp this design of mine," Praful continued. I've already submitted one of my research publications on this issue to a reputable international magazine. As a result, as soon as my paper on this design is published in a few months, you can read it and gain additional clarity!" Then he tried to console Sarvesh by claiming he would assist him whenever he needed it, but not on Ayan's project. As a result, this meeting was of no practical value to Sarvesh. He was right back where he started!

With the constraints at hand, Sarvesh began to devote even more time to comprehnd this design by visiting the libraries of Bangalore's top academic institutions and other research organizations. A few months later, he learned of Praful's published work in a reputable journal, but it was of little use because Praful had not divulged any genuine inside specifics of his design in that piece. Only Praful's career profile had improved due to this article's publishing. As a result, Sarvesh's last hope had likewise evaporated. Praful had released his work without authorization from the DWI administration; amazingly, no one had stopped him. Sarvesh, on the other hand, had progressed in terms of comprehending that design throughout the two months of his struggle. After another month, he completed all of the document draftings. He also discovered some fundamental shortcomings in Praful's design after more examination and experimentation. He discussed those aspects with Ayan, but the manager had been uninterested and had merely wanted this work accomplished at whatever cost. Regardless, Sarvesh polished the design by resolving the shortcomings, and the full process had taken him about six months to complete.

Ayan was overjoyed, and all he said was, "Sarvesh, I knew you would do this one day!" Sarvesh, on the other hand, was unimpressed and unmotivated by this gesture. He deserved a lot more credit because this was one of the department's most important tasks, and he had accomplished it all by himself, despite being a new engineer fresh out of college. Ayan received true recognition, while Sarvesh's name stayed in the background. Mr Madhav, the department head, also forgot to notice Sarvesh's work. Madhav had been on good terms with both Rozy and Praful, from the time they were dating each other. Ayan never mentioned Sarvesh's name in front of senior management. Sarvesh had no idea that he had to struggle for his rightful recognition back then. He was raised in the old school, and he respected the elders. Ayan was promoted to the next level and given more projects due to his self-advertised achievement on that project.

During this time, DWI received one key project from ACTR (i.e., Advanced Consortium of Telecom Research), Germany, which was a prominent research organisation in that country. This project was a collaborative work between DWI and ACTR. Based on the recent success of Sarvesh's project, Ayan's name was chosen to lead that project. In fact, Ayan had never really bothered to highlight Sarvesh's name as against his own. As a result, Ayan travelled to Germany for that project as well. When he returned from that place after a few months, he told Sarvesh one fine day that he was quitting DWI for good and relocating to Germany with his family. Sarvesh later learned that Ayan had used that particular trip to his advantage and had already arranged some soft agreement with important personnel at ACTR, allowing him to relocate to that country seamlessly. During this time, it was a topic of conversation in one of the departmental gossip about how Ayan had benefited much from Sarvesh's hard work. Ayan's career had been catapulted to new heights due to it.

Anyway, on the last working day of Ayan's departure, the department head Madhav threw a small party, and everyone had a fantastic time. Sarvesh sang a farewell song on that occasion at the request of colleagues, and it was only then that people recognized he had a wonderful voice and was a fantastic singer. One of the other managers joked that Sarvesh could try his luck in Bollywood rather than pursuing a corporate career! Sarvesh gradually lost touch with Ayan once he moved away, as there was no efficient form of communication back then like there is now with social media. Furthermore, in the modern day, Praful and Rozy are well-established in the USA. DWI was a stepping stone for these individuals, and they had reaped significant benefits from their time here and done everything necessary to advance their careers. Today, it appears that they had meticulously plotted their professional path, largely at the expense of Sarvesh's hard work. In any case, there is a saying that one is given even more labor with every success. Sarvesh experienced the same thing. Because he had re-created, validated, improvised, and corrected someone else's preliminary design, this initial project work had given him a lot of steam to deal with the more difficult problems. As a result, Sarvesh thanks God now that he has grown stronger due to this experience. However, he still wishes someone had noticed his efforts, as it would have been a good recognition. Regardless, he gradually forgot about the incident over time and continued to take on and complete increasingly difficult duties within the organization.

Chapter-3

Love in the Air

When Sarvesh finished his first major assignment in his department, his fellow DWI batch mates were experimenting with new projects in their respective departments. Their managers allotted them a lot of time to read and learn in the DWI library and gradually contribute. So, they were wondering about Sarvesh's overwork in his first assignment. They were even skeptical that they would go through such a difficult period in their own departments, but that apprehensive thought never came true while at DWI.

During one of the lighter moments in library talks amongst the batch mates, one of the girls asked Sarvesh if he wanted to join her to go to a singing class near the office. Getting a formal music education in Bangalore was a good idea, which was one of the main Carnatic music hubs. She was from southern India. Sarvesh was naturally interested in Hindustani vocal classes because he was from northern India. So they went to the classes but attended separate teacher's lessons due to their interests. Something interesting happened during this time. Sarvesh's singing talent had already made him popular among his batch mates, and he frequently sang at small get-togethers. Someone mentioned one day that a girl named Manjari in the GET batch was a fantastic singer. Sarvesh became interested in her, and the next day in the office cafeteria, he happened to meet Manjari when she came to meet her friend. This friend of Manjari was the same girl who was attending the music class with Sarvesh. Both these girls shared the same linguistic background and were both from the southern Indian state of Andhra Pradesh.

Manjari had a charming appearance and humble demeanor, which many would like to see in a traditional Indian girl with a good family upbringing. She had a twinkle in her eyes and a very down-to-earth demeanor. She had long, thick hair and a small black Bindi (a colored dot or sticker) on her forehead. It enhanced her beauty. She resembled an old Hindi film actress. She had learned classical music since she was a child. Sarvesh was drawn to her from within the moment he saw her. But he never expressed his feelings to her. She extended her hand for a handshake to Sarvesh during their first meeting in the friends' group. Sarvesh felt genuine warmth in her greeting. Other male friends were envious of Sarvesh's musical ability at the time. Manjari mentioned that she was already aware of his singing talent and would like to sing duet songs with him at future DWI events. Sarvesh was pleasantly surprised by her speed of friendly association with someone he had only met a day before. Anyway, he approved of her, and they both went about their business for the day.

On one of the late evenings, Sarvesh was alone in his LAB, completing some experiments, long after his department colleagues had left for the day. He was so engaged in his work that he had lost count of time. Suddenly, he heard a very soft and pleasant voice saying, "Kumar ji, good evening," which helped him to come to terms. Sarvesh was on the verge of being attentive, but not totally. "Hello, Kumar ji; I'm Manjari," said the voice once more. He regained his composure and welcomed her with astonishment at that point. Sarvesh's LAB was on the seventh floor, while hers was on the third. He had almost forgotten about their conversation a few days before. It was unusual for a female colleague to visit his LAB late evening. In his department, most of his coworkers were guys, and they were much older than he was. He was the newest addition to the group and the sole bachelor. At that hour, Sarvesh was not expecting Manjari at his department's LAB. Normally, all-female coworkers would leave the workplace by 6 pm, but it was already 8 pm. So he inquired about her well-being before attempting to deduce the reason for her unexpected visit to his LAB. She explained to him that the administrative officer, Ms. Aruna, had just contacted her that evening and asked if she might perform some cultural singing at the 15th Annual Day of DWI, which was coming up in a month. Manjari also informed him that she had already agreed to perform a Duet Singing performance with him. Also, she had just given her and his names to the administrative officer because there was no time to think about it. As a result, Manjari had rushed to the LAB to obtain his consent and beg pardon for not being able to obtain his permission when giving his name!

She grinned at him with a mischievous expression, yet her countenance revealed a guilty feeling. She was expecting that Sarvesh would forgive her. He was aware of the situation and assured her he would not let her down. She offered to accompany him for dinner at the DWI cafeteria, which he accepted. Both of them chatted about their musical interests over the dinner table. Sarvesh's talent to sing Kishore Kumar's (i.e., the Bollywood's great late legendary singer) romantic numbers nearly identically to the original was already known to her at the time. Shall we sing the song "Kora kagaz tha yeh mann mera, likh diya naam ispe tera?" she said. This song was also an all-time favorite of Sarvesh. He had never heard her sing before, so he requested if she could give a demonstration of her singing. She agreed like a good student and asked him where to go for the Demo. The two decided and walked to the office's Music Room, meant for such practice sessions. No one was around in the office at that late hour, except the security personnel.

It was now 9 pm, and they'd finished their meal. Sarvesh had to skip dinner at home that night, so he dialed his home number from the workplace landline and notified his mother of his late arrival. Staying in the workplace after 9 pm was unusual back then, and it was also raining that night. Both of them proceeded to the music room to look for cassettes, and luckily, one of those cassettes had this song on it. We're talking about a time when the Google search engine wasn't available, and hence there were no lyrics or internet music for them to listen to. As a result, they had to manually play the tape and listen to the music a few times in the player. Both of them prepared their song stanzas and began practicing them. They became used to each other after approximately 15 to 20 minutes and began to sing their parts.

After hearing Manjari's singing for the first time, Sarvesh remarked that she had a lovely voice and that her singing technique was similar to that of Lata Mangeshkar (i.e., the great Bollywood singing Legend who is honoured with the highest civilian award in the country.). Manjari, on the other hand, claimed that she preferred Asha Bhosle's (i.e., another great singer and sister of Lata Mangeshkar) songs to Lata's. She was spellbound the minute Sarvesh sang his stanza and informed him, "Kumar ji, I am an immediate fan of yours and will be a life-long lover of your voice." I haven't seen Kishore Kumar, but I think you are the great Kishore Da, for me! I adore your voice, the range, the confidence with which you sing, the clarity with which you sing, and everything about your singing performance. Whenever we have an opportunity to perform for office parties and gatherings, we shall be singing partners. Please don't forget about me," she added. Sarvesh said to her at this point that he also enjoyed her singing. However, she told him he was much ahead of hers in terms of sheer feeling and expressions in the voice. The first practice session concluded.

That night, they rode in the same cab home and had a fantastic time talking about music and life during the ride. Manjari showed a sense of companionship to Sarvesh on that trip. She talked a lot continuously about many things about her DWI work-life and how she was delighted to be associated with him. At some point during that conversation, she also felt emotional like a kid and revealed that she had lost her father in her childhood. Her mother had raised her and educated her to such a point. Probably, she was getting the warmth of association from Sarvesh that she was mentioning her personal details to him. That song of Kishore Kumar was his father's favourite song, and he used to always sing that song to her mother when he was still alive. As per her confession, whenever she heard that song through Sarvesh's voice, she felt an unexpressed fondness towards him and she had tears in her eyes. Subsequently, over the next few days, they had to perform their song in front of the symphony team, who would be judging their performance. As a result, they repeated the practice with the music beat a few more times after work hours during the next few days.

Over the next month, they met at various workplace locations and discussed things such as life, family, music, their separate cultures, and so on. They had already become excellent friends and had mutual regard for each other; it would not be an exaggeration to state. They used to have a glittering spark in their respective eyes whenever they met. Sarvesh used to feel embarrassed whenever others noticed them together, but Manjari told him not to worry too much about it. They gradually demonstrated their singing abilities to the orchestra team, who enjoyed their pairing and mutual understanding while singing. To do something on stage, it is critical to have this understanding. Even though they were singing well, the Orchestra team informed them that this song was a little slow and urged them to choose another song that was a little faster in terms of pace. Sarvesh was irritated by the last-minute modification. Manjari, on the other hand, consoled him and asked him to choose another song. Fortunately, he discovered a faster song in a very short time. That song appealed to them, and they quickly practiced and perfected it again.

On the day of the Annual Day event, a large auditorium filled with over a thousand DWI colleagues and their families. Sarvesh's parents were present as well. Before the singing performance, he introduced Manjari to his parents, and she accepted their blessings. Sarvesh admired her humility and respect for elders. Their singing performance was the evening's highlight, and they became overnight celebrities. Everyone met them and complimented them, including the company's Managing Director. While Manjari credited Sarvesh for everything, he also complimented her. Later, they performed at many small and large events within DWI, as well as get-togethers and picnic parties. Their friends constantly requested that they perform something for special occasions, and they never let them down. This continued for the next two years until Manjari was in DWI. They regularly visited each other's floors and LABs for the next two years. It was often so uncomfortable for them that even when they went to each other's LABs for work-related problems, people would ask them to sing some songs, which was sometimes awkward. Some even joked about whether or not their relationships were more than just music! But they both realized they treasured their mutual relationship the most.

Sarvesh completed his probation in the year 2002, and his parents gradually but steadily began to pressure him to marry. They were concerned because he was young and they had seen Manjari and him together. According to them, it was possible that he would become distracted by the big city life and marry a girl from a different caste, state, or linguistic background. They had assumed that in such a scenario, it would endanger their well-being in their old age and jeopardize Pramod's career and studies. Sarvesh's elder sister and her family were also heavily reliant on him, and his misstep could hurt their lives and well-being. They had no idea how attached Sarvesh was to the responsibility of his parents and siblings. He was doing everything he could for them, even sacrificing his wishes and desires for their sake. His parents had already begun to consider how to make him feel responsible from a family standpoint and start his own family. They'd also begun to do their homework in the background.

During this process, Sarvesh met Shalini while on his trip to his native place the following summer. This meeting was arranged as a result of their respective parents' discussions. Sarvesh had met a few more girls during that trip as part of his native's arranged marriage process. However, in Shalini, he discovered simplicity, innocence, genuine inner beauty, respect for seniors, and many other qualities that he could not find in others. This first meeting was so intense that they felt they had been waiting for each other for eternity! Sarvesh has been married to Shalini for nearly twenty years now, and they have two daughters together; however, he still believes it was the best thing that ever happened to him. Shalini's voice was husky but soothing, and her natural innocence had stumped him on the first day. Her father was a government employee, and the family was well-to-do and well-known in the city and their circles. Shalini was known to be a very educated girl who consistently excelled in her studies, but she was genuinely humble and an introvert. She had a brown complexion and was in good adult health.

They married in the summers and moved to Bangalore the following week. Sarvesh had arranged two months of internship training in another department at DWI for her academic project. As a result, they used to ride their bike to work, every day. It was a wonderful experience for both of them because he had only recently learned to ride a bike. Those three months as a magical time in their newlywed lives. Shalini had to spend a lot of time in the DWI library at the beginning for her project work and literature studies. She would occasionally run into some of Sarvesh's coworkers, including Manjari.

Manjari happened to meet Shalini and Sarvesh in the library one day, and she immediately greeted Shalini with warmth and praised Sarvesh in front of her for his singing, as well as wished both of them good luck in life. Sarvesh gradually became preoccupied with family matters after his regular office hours, and life was delightful with Shalini. Seasons passed this way, and they both enjoyed the Bangalore weather and life together. They both were young and innocent and in many ways, they grew together.

Chapter-4

The Next Phase

It was 2004-05, and Sarvesh had established himself in his department. Around this time, he began to report to another new manager. Another significant event occurred when DWI was awarded a completely new and advanced wireless product development project from a reputable and respected customer organization. This project, however, was assigned to a different DWI department. Sarvesh was disappointed that his department's personnel had not done enough to bring this project to the team. He had some friends in that other department. From them, he used to get some general information about what was going on.

One day, his seniors informed him that the project had been assigned to them because the key person in the other department, Mr Umang, was leaving the organization. Umang was a bright young man from Tamil Nadu and widely regarded as the most knowledgeable about the projects he was in charge of. He was almost ten years senior to Sarvesh. His department was not in a position to complete that project when he left. At this point, Sarvesh's department team became active and attempted to take over the project knowledge transfer from him. So, on paper, the seniors' names were highlighted to upper management for them to own and execute that high-profile project. Sarvesh's name was never mentioned, even though the actual execution of work came slowly to him. People in the department began to take on knowledge transfer and work handover during the transition period of Umang's departure.

Several meetings were scheduled between Umang and Sarvesh's superiors. Sarvesh was invited to some of the discussions and not to others. Initially, it appeared that the seniors on his team understood what needed to be done and that they could complete it. However, it became clear over time that this project required a significant amount of technical substance and effort from individuals, which neither Umang nor the seniors possessed at the time. Apparently, neither Umang nor Sarvesh's seniors had completed the technology assessment in a proper way either. They had undertaken this activity solely because the project had been assigned to them without conducting any thorough gap analysis. They were overly reliant on third-party vendors to complete this work for them. However, even external vendors did not have the necessary knowledge back then. As a result, the job dragged on, and deadlines were missed.

One fine day, the new manager approached Sarvesh and asked him to take on some critical aspects of this project for which no one had the necessary knowledge or experience. Sarvesh did not have the required knowledge for that high-end, technology-rich task at the time. This time, he had access to many documents and files about Umang's work, but after studying them, he realized that Umang had tried his hand at everything but had no firm grasp on the actual work because the technology was new, Umang did not have the necessary knowledge. He appeared to have been attempting to create something beyond his capabilities. But he was at least trying, and his work showed that he had failed numerous times, and the bits and pieces of his work were half-completed or had not yet begun. At times, he had tried some crude methods of achieving the results. Here, a systematic approach and planning were severely lacking. Many of his documents were disorganized.

When this task was assigned to Sarvesh, his department seniors had most likely realized the difficulty and did not want to put any more effort into it, so they transferred this work to Sarvesh's bucket to complete. So it became clear that regardless of the nature or phase of this project, he would be the executor while the seniors would be officially responsible. The seniors had taken on a hugely complex task for their career advancement without proper handover or analysis. They were faking it for name recognition, promotion, etc. Anyway, he took on this primary difficult task for the second time in this organization, and it was even more difficult this time. He expressed his concerns to Shalini, who stated, "Sarvesh, I do not understand your technical work, but I know you can only do this, and so God has given it to you." "During this time, I am by your side. We'll get through." Sarvesh was concerned that he would be spending more time at the office, including weekends, for this job, which would entail a lot of personal sacrifice from family time. However, in Shalini, he found both a very understanding wife and a dearest friend. She inspired him to get to the bottom of the problem and solve it from the ground up, even if it meant putting in more effort. She advised him to do everything possible and not leave any stone unturned.

During this period, also few junior engineers were hired through campus placement, many of whom came from prestigious universities. A couple of them were assigned to Sarvesh's department. With his manager's approval, he gave them some of the regular tasks. They lacked the skills to perform high-end technical tasks, so he assigned them lower-level tasks, de-linked himself from the generic tasks, and focused on the critical functions. One of the primary tasks necessitated extensive research and detailed studies of current literature and practical implementations carried out by others worldwide. This was during the early days of the Google search engine when technical information was not yet widely available to the general public. As a result, literature on actual practical implementation was scarce. As a result, the more he tried to delve into the high-end design aspects of Umang's half-cooked work, the more obstacles and frustrations he encountered. He also tried calling Umang. But unlike Praful, he was honest and told him that this type of work 'know-how' was not available in India. As per him, only a few people or organizations in the world could do justice to this type of work implementation. As a result, he believed it would take more time and investigation, with sincerity. He was correct because the technology was still in its early stages and had not yet matured. However, there were no excuses to be idle on this matter alone.

Sarvesh accepted the challenge and tried even harder, not afraid of failure. Some pessimists in the department were constantly telling him that it was impossible to implement that type of work because it required global exposure. Sarvesh, on the other hand, was very clear in his understanding of the importance of the work involved. According to his assessment, even if this advanced technology project was new, some fundamental implementation aspects must have been linked to legacy military applications. As a result, he continued to look for relevant sources in several top libraries across India. He was in the FR & IC (i.e., Fundamental Research and Information Communications) institute library one Saturday afternoon during the weekend, for some literature survey. He suddenly came across one of the defense wireless journals' old research papers from 1955. One of the pioneers of those years published an interesting article in this journal. It had some resemblance to the DWI wireless project.

Sarvesh immediately jumped up with joy as it gave him a ray of hope. However, that paper was implemented using outdated technology and focused on theoretical aspects. In any case, something was available for him to investigate further. He spent a few more days analyzing and studying the theory's complexities before creating a full pen-paper-based practical implementation design. As the nature of the work was in another hardware platform, he made several changes to the original theory. Then he used the Software tools to simulate his design, and the results were very encouraging. Furthermore, he implemented the actual hardware prototype and tested it. The test results were very satisfying and corresponded to the fundamental concepts. He became ecstatic about the results and the process he had followed thus far. As a result, he continued his subsequent advanced work and constructed several more complex works. Finally, 8-10 months after the project was assigned to him; he was able to deliver working hardware that could be shown to higher management at DWI. This design was incorporated into the overall product, and the result was highly successful. Sarvesh also shared his success story with Umang, who was astounded by how quickly and effectively Sarvesh achieved his goals! Sarvesh thanked Shalini for her unwavering personal support during this challenging time, as she was the only person who remained emotionally present for him. She was correct about the final result because she had predicted it. By this point, he had gained enough courage and experience to take on more challenging tasks.

During this time, the previous department head retired, and a new leader took over the department; nevertheless, it quickly became apparent that this new leader was incapable of handling the burden of managing large and complex projects. At this point, many employees had already left the organization. Suddenly, Sarvesh's immediate manager also departed from the company, and the new department head was making a massive mess of things. As a result, Sarvesh did not receive much recognition for the months of hard work he had put in. Gradually, he became demotivated due to the new department head's indifferent attitude and discouraging nature. A piece of unfavorable information also reached him around that time. He learned that the new department head had blocked his career promotion since Sarvesh was not in his inner group! Sarvesh was always focused on his profession and never tried to be closer to someone for pity's sake. He had always hoped his labor would earn him the acclaim he deserved, but this was not the case. Even though he had performed exceptionally well on his responsibilities, exceeding all expectations, the organization had not done him justice.

These most recent happenings left him utterly distraught. At the time, very few of his close friends were left in DWI with whom he could discuss this problem. Hence, one day, Sarvesh resigned from his job. At that time, the DWI Director spoke with Sarvesh and attempted to persuade him to continue. Still, Sarvesh understood that the ground reality would remain demoralizing for him, as his friends and batch mates had already received promotions with less effort. Slowly, he noticed that his resume was attracting positive attention from some of the world's largest MNCs, including Unikue Wireless Tech (UWT), USA. After leaving DWI, he worked with them for the following three to four years.

By the time Sarvesh presented his DWI job experience to Marc H., he was pleased with Sarvesh's approach and management of technical challenges in his first organization. In addition, he admired that, at such a young age, he had the maturity and unyielding but adaptable mentality to rise to the occasion and deliver during difficult stages. That morning, he asked a few more technical questions, which Sarvesh answered exceptionally well. The interview was a success, and he told Sarvesh, "I'm pleased with your interview; please be prepared for the second round." I wish you success in that round as well. This was mentioned with a smile, and the meeting concluded on a friendly note.

Chapter-5

In Between Hope and Happiness

Sarvesh was pleased with his performance in the first round of interviews and immersed himself in his daily activities. At the breakfast table, he informed Shalini about his interview, and they briefly discussed the flashbacks that occurred throughout the transitions from DWI to UIDC. In Chennai, Unikue Wireless Tech's India Development Center (UIDC) was a joint venture between Kredilo Info Systems (KIS) and Unikue Wireless Tech (UWT). Unlike KIS, an Indian I.T. giant UWT was an American company with headquarters in Irvine, California. The KIS team established the Offshore Development Center (ODC) for UWT in Chennai. The operations of this ODC were entirely controlled by UWT, resulting in a system like that of a multinational corporation (MNC). As he spoke with her, he was flooded with thoughts of those days. His recollection of those days was quite distressing. That day, Shalini made DOSAs in the Chennai style, and he suddenly recalled his days in Chennai.

It was difficult for him to leave his R&D job in Bangalore, and his own home. At the time, he had recently constructed his home in Bangalore. His father wanted him to build a home for the entire joint family in Bangalore, as he was well-established in that reputable organization. At that time, his older brother did not have a job and was re-starting his college education again, but he was already married and had a little child. He and his family were dependent on Sarvesh. His sibling needed additional space for his growing family and wanted to devote more time to his studies. Understanding his father's and brother's needs, Sarvesh constructed this home. For the construction of this home, he secured a bank loan based on his earning capacity and collateral. As much effort had gone into developing that house, he was highly emotional about leaving it and his secure employment. Ironically, certain persons at DWI influenced his choice to leave that organization.

At the time, he had two young children. The older was three years old, while the younger was only a few months old. Shalini was immensely concerned with day-to-day household obligations and children, so she was not involved in his choice to leave DWI. Consequently, when he informed her of this, she was concerned about his transitions to a new job and city. At the time, his eldest child was attending nursery school in Bangalore, and she had just begun to like it. In this circumstance, Sarvesh felt bad for placing his wife and children in a tough situation. Whenever this notion enters his mind, he experiences a heavy feeling of guilt. Even though Shalini was not in the best of moods to leave Bangalore, she had little choice but to comply with him, given the circumstances.

After talking with his parents and older brother, Sarvesh made career-related transition options. They were both completely aware of the situation. Since Sarvesh's income was about to rise, they were unconcerned about Shalini's other difficulties. Most of DWI's workforce consisted of long-term personnel who typically retired after decades of service. There was stability in the job, till the retirement age. However, Sarvesh had to quit that job. He was also going to move his wife and children to a new place with many unknowns.

Around that time, Sarvesh had floated his bio-data to a few job search websites, and many opportunities came his way. However, he liked the job, which was from Chennai city, and it was the job offer from the UIDC. That company planned to hire local talents to execute the work from Chennai and also to support India-based customers. Sarvesh had got his interviews cleared very effectively due to his excellent work at DWI, and the experience had helped him a lot. The UWT interview panelists were super-impressed with his knowledge base. They had not expected that someone in India could know such advanced technology-related practical implementations. The global Manager, Nitin, had invited him to travel to the USA and Norway immediately after joining them. That offer was fascinating for him and his family. Sarvesh could better support his brother financially due to this new job's enhanced financial position. Hence, they had motivated him to look forward, not bothering about the past. However, he was going to miss the lifelong job security of the DWI.

As soon as he got this new job, his brother's desires skyrocketed as he could immediately enrol himself in advanced job-oriented training programs.

Subsequently, these training and certifications enhanced his brother Pramod's employability and earning capacity later. Before that, Pramod had just completed his academic degree in computers in Bangalore. It is ironic to mention here that during Sarvesh's engineering studies, he struggled with his basic needs of food, books, etc., as his father was running a loss-making business to survive. But now, Sarvesh made sure that his elder brother did not have to suffer for his studies, even if Pramod could not support Sarvesh during his studies. One can say that Sarvesh was doing more than what a genuine and ideal brother does to his siblings. Actually, in normal cases, the elder brothers support their younger brothers in various ways but, here was an uncommon scenario wherein a sincere younger brother was shaping the career and life of his elder brother and brother's family! It would be on another topic what Sarvesh got in return from his extended family members like brothers and sister. This job-oriented high-cost training program helped Pramod a lot to get a better job in an MNC in Chennai.

On the work front, with this new job, Sarvesh got an opportunity to work with new technologies and some global engineers. So, he tried to forget the workplace associated with bad memories from his previous organization. Hence, with these entire contexts, as soon as he got the job offer, he accepted that immediately and started planning his travel to the Chennai work location. The new job required him to work primarily out of Chennai, but he was expected to travel to UWT's other geographical office locations to get involved in different projects. The plan was to get the knowledge base to India and set up those kinds of lab and testing facilities in their Chennai office. So, Sarvesh resigned from DWI on one fine day and booked a train ticket to Chennai with his family. Since his parents and brother's family depended heavily on him for day-to-day survival related to basic needs and education, they also travelled to Chennai. Sarvesh had booked the 2nd A.C. train tickets for them as well.

After reaching Chennai, he rented a bigger house for all the family members to stay in. He always cared for the needs of his brother and parents very much. He was very much attached to them and respected them hugely; many times, he sacrificed his own needs to fulfil their wants and wishes. The train travel was arranged quickly, and the new company hardly gave him any time to relax. The company people were so impressed by his profile that they wanted him to join them as soon as possible and work with them. Anyhow, one fine morning in that rainy season, the train reached Chennai, and all the family members started to settle there for a few years to come.

While Sarvesh was navigating the past in a flash at the breakfast table, the Whizwin Corp HR, Jay, called him. He informed Sarvesh that Marc H was impressed with his interview and that the next round would be scheduled the next day. Sarvesh agreed and went about his business for the rest of the day. Shalini was overjoyed that day because he had done well in the interview. Anyway, his next interview was scheduled with another man named Andy Campos. He worked as a Design Director in the new company's USA office. Because of his recent interview experience, Sarvesh had begun to look into the non-technical aspects of his CV. The interview was scheduled for the following evening, India time.

Andy had a happy face but a witty outlook, and whenever he spoke, he related work and life lessons very closely. He quickly reviewed Sarvesh's profile and asked, "Sarvesh, you are already working in a reputed Indian organization [i.e., Imagyne Tech]. Why are you looking for a change?" Sarvesh stated that having previously worked with global organizations, he was interested in working with a global workforce and diversity again. Andy's next question was, "Can you please explain in your career path some scenarios and case studies when you had made such a transition from an Indian organization to a global organization and successfully handled the transition?" This question was appropriate for Sarvesh to talk about his job transition from DWI to UIDC, which occurred almost a decade ago.

September marked the beginning of Sarvesh's transition to his new job in Chennai. His family resided in a sub-urban section of Chennai city, and he commuted to work using public transportation and a suburban railway. He has not previously purchased any personal vehicles in Chennai. Due to this, he would leave for work early in the morning and return home late at night, having had a long and exhausting workday. He was the first individual to join that team as a leader, and at about the same time, Sarvesh mentored another engineer who had joined the group. He was Sarvesh's junior, and his name was Madhukar. He was in good health and exhibited much cleverness in his conversations and work conduct. He arrived at the office at 10 am and left at 6 pm. According to the team manager's arrival and departure times, he would come and depart the office precisely on time. He was such a cunning individual that he consistently arrived 15 minutes before the KIS manager, Kavi, in the morning and left 10 minutes after the boss's departure. Not sure how he managed to accomplish that. Even if the client gave him extra work, he would manipulate it so that he would never be overworked for more than seven to eight hours each day, regardless of the circumstances.

As the project's leader, Sarvesh was obligated to shoulder this additional load, as Kavi had a habit of placing the entire burden on his shoulders while the group was young and expanding. Kavi felt confident that Sarvesh would take care of the team's job due to his sincerity. Kavi was married and about 15 years older than Sarvesh. He lacked a solid technical background. Technically, he was dependent on Sarvesh. Even though he had been married for so long, he did not have any children with whom he could spend time; yet, he would leave the office at 6 pm. every day. Later, Sarvesh learned that Kavi was a guy of many hues and hobbies, including real estate, horseback riding, swimming, talking with female colleagues, etc. He had a bushy moustache and a pessimistic exterior demeanour. His health was normal, and he always spent more time gossiping with his peer-level managers at the workplace than on actual work. Since he lacked proficiency in technical matters, he made no substantial contribution to the team's development. Instead, he believed in forming alliances with others who shared his own native state's linguistic background. He has always considered native speakers of his language to be the most remarkable and talented individuals on the planet. As a result, he mostly hired native-language-speaking engineers. He would often address them in their native language in the presence of others, creating an environment that was often offensive to others who did not understand what he was saying.

In most multinational corporations and organizations, personnel must be neutral regarding language, race, etc. However, Kavi was highly biased toward his native language, and everyone in the team disliked this trait of his greatness. However, no one ever spoke about this. Moreover, since he maintained an excellent relationship with the upper management team, he had the freedom to accomplish various tasks of his choice. He used to attend client meetings but would place responsibility on the shoulders of others. When Sarvesh first joined the group, Kavi did his best to maintain a cheerful demeanour; nonetheless, he was deeply anxious about Sarvesh's presence because he was highly dependent on him technically, yet he did not want Sarvesh to stand out. Since he could not manage the team without Sarvesh, he did his best to keep him busy and overburdened with several client-related tasks so that he never had time to think about anything other than work. He was extremely tolerant in giving leaves of absence to the majority of the group who spoke his native language. Others could recognize these details, but Sarvesh never gave a second thought to them, except for the work itself.

On the day he joined this organization, Sarvesh completed general paperwork with the H.R. and Finance teams and then met with Kavi, in the afternoon. He greeted Sarvesh with a sly smile and a controlled attitude evident in his external appearance. In an email, he presented him to the UWT managers and briefed him on his primary role of assuming all the pending essential technical duties. Before that, another female employee performed a tiny amount of ad hoc labour. She was completely unaware of the domain work, but Kavi had convinced the client to train her so that gradual progress could be made until Sarvesh arrived. By the time Sarvesh arrived, she had already squandered a great deal of time and was not at all productive, and the quality of her work was pitiful. In reality, he had to undo all of her previous labour, and the client was becoming impatient for the work to be completed because so much time had already been lost.

Therefore, he spent additional hours correcting her errors and attempting to get the entire project to a satisfactory, client-acceptable level of completion. The client was pleased with Sarvesh's first week's worth of work. The client instructed Kavi to send Sarvesh and Madhukar on a three-month trip to Norway to complete time-sensitive project tasks.

Chapter-6

Even the Sun takes Rest for 12 hours

It was extremely short notice, and Sarvesh had just arrived in Chennai a week prior, so he was still settling in. His children were not yet settled in their schools, and he was suddenly required to make trip arrangements. Madhukar was ecstatic about this trip, but Sarvesh was apprehensive because he needed a few more weeks to settle down before this trip. However, due to the crucial nature of this project, he had to agree with Kavi and the client. Once again, workplace priorities trumped those of his personal life. His parents were pleased with this trip. They, together with Pramod, advised Sarvesh to always look forward and reminded him that he need not worry too much about family concerns because his children were still young, and that was the time for him to take risks, according to their assessment.

Regardless, both Sarvesh and Madhukar obtained their Norwegian VISAs without delay. They traveled to Delhi to obtain this VISA from the Norwegian Consulate. That was Sarvesh's maiden flight on a domestic airline to Delhi. By that point, Madhukar had already flown, as he had shrewdly availed the flight journey through the company reimbursement mode, to join the Chennai office. He also managed to obtain Kavi's approval for that trip. However, at the time of joining UIDC, Sarvesh had to travel by train mode, along with his parents, brother and his brother's wife and kid. Hence, he could not be selfish to book a flight ticket just for himself, Shalini and their kid. He kept on making these types of sacrifices for the sake of his relatives and failed to understand the happiness of his own family. After a few days after receiving the VISA, he packed his belongings and began his journey to Norway. Even though this country is smaller than some of India's regional states, it was already a developed country with a very high per capita income population.

Sarvesh had reserved a car to drop him off at the airport on a cold winter night in Chennai. His father and brother had accompanied him to the airport. It was a once-in-a-lifetime occurrence for a family member to go outside of India in the entire family history. Due to his son's journey to Europe, his father's social standing rose to a new level. Unaware of these happenings, Sarvesh was extremely upset as he prepared to leave his wife and children for the first time to travel such a long distance for several months. It was like going to a battlefield and was unsure of the outcome and when he would return home. In the middle of the night, his children were asleep, and Shalini shed tears as she watched him go so abruptly. Those tears did not go down well with her in-laws, Umakanth and his wife. Sarvesh was expected to maintain emotional control and urged Shalini to do the same.

In those days, cell phone usage had recently penetrated Indian households, but it was not as ubiquitous as today. Additionally, not everyone could afford to own a phone. It was only utilized for the most vital of causes. He reassured Shalini that he would contact her daily from Norway. Even though he was unsure if he would be able to maintain that promise, he had to tell her so that she would be somewhat consoled and would let him go. Regardless, he had begun driving towards the airport, and he could see Shalini's face excitedly awaiting his return date through the car's windows.

This was his first flight to a remote foreign location outside his native country. Sarvesh had never been on an international flight before, so he would ask the folks surrounding him if he had any doubts. As soon as the plane took off, he felt incredibly upset about leaving the country and his family. After passing through Germany and Frankfurt, the airplane was intended for the Norwegian city of Finnmark. The huge flight had two levels of seating and ten seats in a row. He was appreciative of the flight attendants' professionalism and customer-centric conduct whenever he observed their friendly gestures. That night, after a delicious meal at home, Sarvesh was feeling sleepy and tired. It was a journey of eight hours to Frankfurt. He was already exhausted from the day's events and running around for Forex arrangements, completing and summarising the project operations at the workplace, and then dealing with the family's feelings. As a result, as soon as the plane ascended to tens of thousands of feet, he fell asleep.

It was already daylight, but the airplane was still in the air when he suddenly sensed someone trying to rouse him up. Here stood Madhukar in front of the aisle. Initially, Sarvesh could not see him during the hustle-bustle of the trip and believed that he would arrive on a separate flight. However, it appeared that Madhukar had already fallen asleep in the flight by the time Sarvesh boarded this huge Boeing aeroplane. Thus he was unable to spot him before he boarded. Regardless, he informed Sarvesh that they were close to reaching Frankfurt. As soon as they landed in Frankfurt, the subsequent flight was available within a few hours. This second flight was only two hours in duration. At least there were many Indians on the first flight, but none besides these two males were on the second flight. With all the foreigners surrounding him, Sarvesh began to miss his home country even more.

As usual, Madhukar acted as if he was a seasoned veteran, and he would speak to anyone like a child, causing them to become annoyed. With his terrible English speaking skills, he used to introduce himself to everyone around on that flight, even if no one was interested in him! Sarvesh, on the other hand, was a man of moderation and caution who only spoke to others when necessary. Being a strict vegetarian, Sarvesh could not consume any food on the second flight due to the availability of non-vegetarian options. Sarvesh longed for Indian cuisine and grew homesick for his native cooking. On the other hand, Madhukar had no culinary limits and consumed everything. His philosophy was straightforward: he ate and drank whatever was offered to him for free or sponsored by others, without hesitation. He even consumed alcoholic beverages offered on board. Sarvesh never consumed these drinks.

Finally, the jet landed in Norway around 6 pm local time. Unlike India, this country had a relatively small population, and Sarvesh instantly felt like he was in a magical land on the opposite side of the globe. Surprisingly, the outside sky appeared to be 3 pm even though it was nearly 6 pm. He was curious as to what was happening. Instantaneously, he realized that the particular pattern of day-to-night transitions was caused by Norway's proximity to the North Pole. Consequently, the Sun's beams followed a path that prevented the normal sunset to occur, as it does in India. Both of them hired a taxi to the hotel where they had a reservation. On the way to the hotel, it was a pleasant journey with little traffic, and Sarvesh felt as if he had arrived in a great place, despite the desolate surroundings.

The hotel was situated on the city's outskirts and beside a lake surrounded by winter trees. This city was the location of UWT's factory. This was an important location for the company's production facilities, which were centered there. The hotel provided a tasty complimentary breakfast, cooking facilities for all guests, a sauna, a fitness center, etc. In those days, he was unfamiliar with these facilities. That day, they both settled into the hotel. Then, Sarvesh attempted a Skype call to his residence. Those days, Skype was the only method available for relatively inexpensive long-distance international internet calling. Due to his laptop issues, he could not make a call that day. Subsequently, he went out of the hotel to make an international phone call from a booth. Still, he could not do so because it was a weekend holiday and, unlike in India, weekend evenings were virtually deserted everywhere. Despondent, he returned to the hotel.

He noted that Madhukar was conversing with his family via Skype with great joy. Sarvesh could not disturb him, and also Madhukar did not offer to call him through his laptop. Sarvesh felt extremely bad that he was thousands of kilometers from home and unable to notify his family of his safe arrival in Norway. Madhukar was not at all grateful to Sarvesh inspite of all the help he was getting from him, at work. The quality of the laptops provided by KIS's local I.T. team was subpar. Due to the daily workload and the high expectations of Kavi and the UWT client team to keep the work as a top priority, there was insufficient time to verify their accuracy. Due to the rapid planning of the trip, he did not have sufficient time to confirm the quality of the laptop. In any case, he had to wait until the next day before he could contact home, and only after the Norway I.T. team of UWT had resolved the laptop issue. The company KIS did not supply him with a telephone to call home. These are the fundamental responsibilities that organizations must uphold. However, many corporations focus solely on their business.

After nearly 48 hours of leaving home, Sarvesh felt extremely bad when speaking to his wife and children. They had been quite anxious in the absence of information regarding him for the past two days. It took him considerable time to overcome this reaction, and he was distressed over the KIS team and Manager. Devoted employees like him were seemingly taken for granted. His wife encouraged him to be strong and forget about these challenges, inspiring him to devote himself entirely to his work. She anticipated that he would bounce back irrespective of the challenges in a foreign country.

The following day, he traveled to the new office location of UWT. He was scheduled to handle and complete several difficult and time-sensitive professional assignments in a short period. The Norwegian (i.e., people of Norway) were friendly, but they spoke very little and were intensely devoted to their profession. As he discovered while conversing with the engineers, their skill was exceptional. Consequently, he began to contact them gradually, and with his commitment, he made a positive impression in that office within a short span of time. Nitin, the Manager of UWT in the United States, was extremely pleased by his talent, diligence, professional ethics, and knowledge. Even in Norway, Madhukar presented himself in such a way that he always received a small share of the work. He was showing his inability to do high-end work! Therefore, the client was hesitant to assign him any difficult tasks. Thus, he could reduce his work hours to a maximum of 8 hours. During his time in Norway, he maintained a well-balanced lifestyle. He mostly concentrated on the documentation effort.

Due to Sarvesh's excellent level of professionalism and skill, the client team provided him with a great deal of challenging work that even the local Norwegian engineers could not do! It took him a great deal of time and intuition to design a strategy and coordinate with global teams and vendors in the United States, India, Norway, etc., to complete his work. His daily work schedule spanned the globe's three time zones (i.e., Europe, India, and the USA). While Madhukar could leave the office at 5 pm nearly every day, Sarvesh typically left between midnight and one a.m. It was truly a highly demanding job. The KIS management team had already begun to portray him as the FACE of the KIS and UIDC joint venture when he accepted this task. He could not afford to make a mistake in front of the client's organization. KIS got awarded many subsequent projects due to his excellent performance in Norway. With this, the KIS got benefited immeasurably owing to his tremendous effort, dedication, talent, and professionalism. The client's staff and organization were quite satisfied with his performance. The managers at the U.S. office talked highly of Sarvesh's presence, work ethic, and achievements among his colleagues. He became an instant star among the client company's Senior Directors, VP, and CEO. Thus, KIS received more business, and Sarvesh's work schedule became busier due to extra tasks and obligations. Many of these jobs had also consumed his weekend time. In this manner, time passed slowly.

During the middle of Sarvesh's stay in Norway, the change from the rainy to the winter season occurred, and he consequently experienced a decrease in temperature. Snowfalls in every direction were fascinating and quite lovely. This was his first encounter with this type of atmosphere. At that time, he had purchased a bicycle from a neighborhood market and cycled to work. Since taking a taxi to work had become too expensive, he had begun cycling to work. During the foreign trip, KIS did not pay its employees enough to cover the cost of a daily cab ride to and from work.

After working late night shifts, Sarvesh would ride through a two-kilometer section of dense forest to reach his accommodation. Compared to the suburban highway road, this trip was a bit shorter. Late at night, riding a bicycle on a suburban street was not risk-free, as traffic vans and police officers occasionally stopped cyclists to ask unwanted questions. Therefore, to avoid this, Sarvesh utilized an alternative Forest path to reach the hotel. Frequently, his travel to the hotel in the dead of night was frightening, dark, and solitary. Nearly 5 kilometers separated the office from the accommodation.

One early morning, he had to get to the office for work, so he carefully navigated the snowy, slick roads to get there. A significant snowfall had occurred the previous evening throughout the city, making the ground quite slippery. That morning, he made every effort to arrive at his office by 7 a.m. local time, for some critical work. Initially, he was oblivious that the snow at the entry to the office gate was treacherously slick. Even though he was wearing anti-slip shoes, he became distracted by the bicycle alongside him, slipped in the snow, and severely wounded his legs. Each time he attempted to ascend, he fell back down. He then crawled to the closest spot and somehow managed to get up, grasping a steel gate nearby.

Sarvesh discussed this situation in the Norway office with Hannah, one of the new Intern students, who had only recently joined the team for a brief phase of her academic obligation. As her Mentor, Sarvesh helped her with her internship project. This was an additional responsibility he was required to do in addition to the challenging tasks he was allocated regularly. She was in her mid-twenties and pursuing a master's degree in engineering at the University Engineering College in Norway. Her assigned workspace was adjacent to that of Sarvesh in the lab. When he told her about the situation, she showed great sympathy. Then, she quickly offered that he moves to a neighboring service apartment and avoid making such a long journey to the hotel during the winter.

She saw his facial expressions as he was hesitant to leave the hotel. Then, she compelled him to relocate to a service apartment close to her residence. She drove him to the apartment in her car, negotiated with the apartment's owner, and assisted with the agreement and associated paperwork. All aspects of the relocation were quickly accomplished with her tremendous and sincere assistance. Along with Sarvesh, Madhukar moved into the flat because he could not afford to stay in the hotel alone due to the high cost of the hotel room. Up to that point, both of them shared the accommodation and its expenses.

With the move to the flat, Hannah and Sarvesh began to communicate more frequently about work, Indian and Norwegian culture, university events, food habits, restaurants, and good shopping destinations nearby. She was a dedicated student, but she also strongly desired to become his friend. In a place where he had few acquaintances, Sarvesh likewise enjoyed her association much. She invited him to a variety of hotels for dinner, as well as to the neighbouring shopping malls. Until then, he could not discuss with her about his family in India. She asked Sarvesh to her home on a beautiful evening, and he accepted.

By the time Sarvesh reached Hannah's home that evening, some melodious Spanish music was playing in her home and incidentally, her parents were away. During a lighter moment on that evening, Hannah felt emotionally closer to Sarvesh. She revealed that she was an orphan and was adopted by her present parents. While talking about some incidents in her life, she felt the warmth of caring from Sarvesh. She was in a way already in love with him. Before she was about to express her feelings, Sarvesh missed his wife and kids very much. He revealed that he is missing his lovely wife and two little kids. However, he also mentioned to her that he enjoyed her company for such a brief period. He recommended that they be lifelong friends. Suddenly, Sarvesh realised that she had been attentively listening to him while displaying unexplainable sentiments for him. He felt that she probably did not anticipate him to be a family man at such a young age! She had tears in her eyes as she realized that they would soon be parting ways, either because she had completed her internship or because his return to India was rapidly approaching. The following evening, they exchanged a handshake and then said their goodbyes. Even after Sarvesh arrived in India, they maintained contact for a while, but he eventually lost touch with her due to his work and busy schedule.

Towards the end of Sarvesh's stay in Norway, a noteworthy event warrants discussion. Through this event, readers will understand even more the level of commitment he has shown not just for his profession but also for the entire UIDC team in India. The United States client manager (Mr. Nitin) and the senior director (Mr Mathew Parker) unexpectedly phoned Sarvesh one evening while he was still engrossed with his primary responsibilities. They informed him that a device was becoming obsolete and that, as a result, an entire line of items would become worthless if it was not replaced with a comparable and equivalent component. The deadline was quickly approaching for it. By the time they called him, he was unaware that the India UIDC team had been unable to analyze this element of the details thoroughly. They had also dragged this problem in his absence for many weeks.

The entire Indian team was composed of a few senior and junior guys, some of whom were near the same age as that of Sarvesh. However, it appeared that the team lacked technical depth and could not evaluate the gravity of the pressing issue at hand. They completely mishandled the situation and failed to comprehend the client's urgency. Consequently, the U.S. client manager and his supervisor were compelled to contact Sarvesh immediately. They told him, "Sarvesh, your India colleagues are unable to solve an issue and have made it worse; we need your assistance here to spend some time on this and provide a solution within a week; otherwise, there will be a significant loss of revenue." While discussing the details, Sarvesh stated that he would do everything in his capacity to address the problem. He requested them to give him the flexibility to handle the situation, to which they quickly agreed. They promised him he could do anything to resolve the issue, and they would back him. Sarvesh immediately requested all pertinent information from Nitin, the India team, the end customer, etc.

That day, he spent the entire night contacting his vendor contacts to obtain the necessary tools for this analysis. With the client team's agreement, he acquired the essential tools and materials for this analysis. The following several days, although he worked on his daytime assignments, he spent sleepless nights analyzing the matter to its core. Finally, he provided a detailed answer, a few alternate solutions, a comprehensive proposal, and a recommendation on how to address the issue. The following day, he convened a meeting with Nitin, Mathew, Kavi, and the India team to discuss his findings and proposal. Nitin and Mathew were pleased and amazed with Sarvesh's concept and solution when he presented them with such specifics and facts. He detected a sense of immense relief in their tone, as this remedy ultimately resolved the issue with their end customer. Instantaneously, Sarvesh rose to prominence among the client company and KIS's upper management. He was valued extremely high. Several of his contemporaries were highly envious of his success. Over the subsequent few years of his employment at UIDC, they did everything they could to slander him. However, each time he emerged even stronger.

Chapter-7

A Camel in the Desert

This was near the end of October, the winter was becoming more severe in Norway, and Sarvesh's work on that project was nearing completion. He had informed his family in India that he would be returning shortly. Nitin had also asked him to look into his return trip options at the time. Nitin had also suggested that Sarvesh take a short break so that he could plan his next trip to the USA office around the start of the New Year. As a result, he was eager to return home. He struggled in Norway at the time because of his vegetarian eating habits. He had difficulty surviving in the European country because he didn't even eat eggs. While at UWT's Norwegian office, he was fortunate to find a kind old lady chef in the cafeteria kitchen who used to make some vegetarian cakes just for him. He used to enjoy eating these cakes. He remembered his grandma due to her kind nature and affectionate gesture toward him. She was the most caring chef, and everyone in that office admired her culinary creations.

In his apartment, Sarvesh used to cook vegetarian meals for himself. He and Madhukar would also occasionally cook together and share the food. Madhukar, for the record, was a non-vegetarian who had no reservations about eating the type of European food. He was having a good time in that country. In his spare time, he explored the countryside of Finnmark city, talked with his family, and even went on long sleep cycles to keep him fresh. He had even visited the sauna in the hotel while they were both staying there until recently. He had taken full advantage of all the hotel's amenities while Sarvesh was always immersed in office work. Anyway, Sarvesh was also very excited about his trip back home and looked into ticket options. Also, his younger child's first birthday was approaching, and Sarvesh was delighted that he would be with her on her special day. He used to miss both of his children a lot, but he missed his second child's smiling face even more. He was very happy to be with his family and kids now that he was already in the mood to return to India, following the success of this project. He had promised them they would go for a party in a large hotel or resort in Chennai. His wife and children were waiting eagerly to see him. They missed him a lot in Chennai because they hadn't spent much time together since moving there from Bangalore.

At this point, on one late evening, his U.S.A. manager, Nitin, called, "Sarvesh, I hope you are doing well. I've got both good and bad news for you. Which one would you like to hear first?" "Please tell me the bad news first so I can digest it," Sarvesh replied. "Sarvesh, I'm sorry to say that your trip to India has to be postponed by a month or so at least because we have a very critical situation to address in our Denmark office and I want you to travel there immediately and help us to solve that pressing situation," Nitin explained. I know you're a star on my team, and my boss wants you to be the only one who can do it because he doesn't trust anyone else on the India team right now." Sarvesh felt very sorry for his bad luck that being a dedicated worker was the price he was about to pay and the amount of sacrifice he had to make after hearing this. He had previously informed him of his child's first birthday, and Nitin had also approved his return trip. But now, this unexpected turn had occurred, and Nitin was just trying to save his face.

"What about Madhukar's trip back home?" Sarvesh inquired. Is he returning home, or is he also accompanying me to Denmark?" "Both of you will travel to Denmark, and he will have to return home immediately because his wife is expecting a baby, and Madhukar needs to be around!" Nitin explained. Till that time, Madhukar had never revealed that to him even if they had shared the room for the last few months. Sarvesh realized that Madhukar had already and skillfully managed his case so that he would get his VISA stamped for Denmark while avoiding the challenging and critical work pressures at that new location and would easily escape to India. This short trip of his appeared to be a paid excursion! Sarvesh later discovered that Madhukar's wife's delivery date was never anywhere nearer and at least a couple of months away! Sarvesh, on the other hand, was forced to sacrifice his personal commitments here to satisfy business needs and some individuals' greed. He was not as cunning as Madhukar in escaping the Denmark project-related challenges. People like Madhukar really do well in corporates because, in every organization, there are a handful of people like Sarvesh to shoulder the extra burden!

Not sure what the most sincere and dedicated employees get in their corporate careers eventually! Sarvesh had not been able to answer this question effectively until today. "What is the good news then?" he asked Nitin, now that he was slowly coming to terms with his emotions. "I will be coming to Denmark while you are there, and I will take you to many good places around," Nitin said, smiling. In addition, many India team members, including India manager Kavi, are expected to arrive simultaneously. As a result, I was hoping you could lead the entire team. It will be an excellent opportunity to demonstrate your breadth and depth of knowledge and expertise in front of talented Danish engineers. They are supposed to be the best in your field. This would be an excellent opportunity for you to learn, contribute, and excel in your field of work."

Sarvesh realized that Nitin and Kavi had already done extensive planning and that informing Sarvesh was merely a formality! They had to inform Sarvesh because he was the person they needed to make this trip a commercial success. Sarvesh was already perplexed about the nature of the good and bad news Nitin had just revealed. He couldn't tell Nitin whether he was happy or sad. As a result, he had to plan his trip to Denmark immediately, and his Norway trip ended. He was attempting to gather energy from nature to fight a new challenge unknown to him. He mustered the courage to tell his wife about this. However, he lacked the courage to speak to his children at that point because he didn't know what to say if they asked about his return trip! Later, he learned that Shalini had informed the children, who were upset, but she had consoled herself and the children. When Sarvesh spoke to them later, the children's faces were filled with sadness and innocence. Shalini had comforted Sarvesh during this difficult time and given him the courage to overcome it. After arriving in India, Sarvesh and Shalini planned to visit some holy places. No one else cared about Sarvesh's sacrifice except Shalini. Also, only he understood the sacrifices of Shalini and the kids. The trip to Denmark was about to be even more hectic than the trip to Norway.

He was planning to depart Norway by reserving an affordable plane ticket through the UIDC travel team. However, Mikka, the Manager of the UWT Norway office, informed him that he was very impressed with his performance. Since he had helped them deliver the project early, he would instead book him a business-class ticket to Denmark. He asked his travel booking staff to reserve a business class ticket immediately. Consequently, Madhukar benefited as well, and he and Sarvesh traveled in business class. Slowly, Sarvesh realized, "Some individuals get fortunate, while only a few put in the true effort in life."

The flight landed in Copenhagen, the capital of Denmark, where the UWT office is located. Soon, Sarvesh learned that the office was situated in a hilly area and it was a long train journey from the hotel to the office. It took significant time to travel by train and then on foot to the office in a dangerous mountainous area where snakes were frequently observed on the route to the station. People who did not own a vehicle or even who did not want to use their own vehicles used to take the train and pedestrian route to the office. During this time, he learned that the India team would be arriving the following day and the KIS team had arranged for an apartment. During that trip, Kavi stayed in a separate luxury condo with a single room while everyone else shared accommodations. Through a reliable source, Sarvesh learned that Kavi and his wife had arrived in Denmark a week ago. However, before the arrival of the remaining team members, he had successfully sent back his wife to India after a leisurely visit to Denmark. Now he was pretending that he had come to lead this team to success. Actually, he had only been there for a couple of days.

The team had at least fifteen members. Now, they all resided in a shared flat. In response to their request, Sarvesh joined and stayed with them. The apartment was an older structure, and apple trees were located behind it. With all the members crammed into that apartment, there was a great deal of chaos in the kitchen because so many people wanted to try their hands at cooking. It was, at times, much more puzzling. During this trip, there were numerous meetings, and all these activities were consuming a lot of Sarvesh's time and energy. Sarvesh was given a long list of work responsibilities, and Nitin asked him to coach the India squad and the remaining team based in India. As a result of UWT's recent acquisition of that Denmark office, the environment was tense, as many employees were departing the organization. The India team was instructed to get the knowledge handover in an expedited manner. Many members of the India team lacked maturity while interacting with customer teams, resulting in numerous unpleasant situations. There were also many non-vegetarians, so Sarvesh had to struggle significantly for food, and his health continued to deteriorate.

During this period, Sarvesh completed the challenging responsibilities set for him. However, by then, he had begun to miss his family, as it had been about three months since he had left India, and his days at the Denmark office were highly stressful. Duc to overwork, his eating and sleep cycles were severely affected. His health was already in a deteriorating phase. He was working like an efficient machine. It would not be incorrect to say that he was skillfully thrown into this situation. This is comparable to a Camel's situation in the desert. A Camel sometimes ends up eating thorns for food in the desert and bleeds in its mouth. It then sucks that blood, believing that it is some delicious and wonderful food! The Camel, forgetting its pain, enjoys the situation and is unaware that it is its blood! Sarvesh, a loyal and dedicated employee, was similarly trapped by Kavi, Nitin and the management of KIS team in such a situation. He was already bleeding in his personal life and health, but he seemed to relish the challenge. Later, he visited some locations in Denmark with Nitin and others but did not enjoy their company. They were fresh with energy while he was stressed out due to the long trip he had been so far. He felt terrible for missing his child's first birthday, and his child's health was in poor condition at the time. They also appeared to miss him greatly. His younger daughter was very much connected to dad, and hence was becoming even more restless in his absence.

After completing his project job in Denmark, Sarvesh ultimately returned home. After a brief break in India, Nitin invited him to Canada on the day of his return. Sarvesh consented, but he became ill for two weeks upon his return to India due to overwork during his recent trip to Europe. Therefore, he could not fly to Canada immediately, despite the approval of his Canada VISA. After returning home, Sarvesh required vitamin injections due to his extreme weakness and illness. His wife and children excitedly awaited his return, while his brother and extended family members waited to see what gifts he brought back from his trip abroad. He gave out all of the gifts to them. The happiness on his child's face was beyond description. His younger child just ran up to him and tightly hugged him. Indeed, it was an emotional moment. In India, Sarvesh took his wife and children on a local trip to the Tirupati temple, an experience that is still fresh in his mind. The children enjoyed the outing immensely. His parents, brother and his family were also there on that trip, as usual, and that trip was sponsored by Sarvesh.

Chapter-8

"How Many Like You Are There?"

Time flew by, in the blink of an eye. It was 2008 when Sarvesh learned that another prospective client, Mr. Atkin, was visiting KIS to discuss potential projects. On that day of the client's visit, Shalini had advised Sarvesh in the morning to wear his lucky dress, and he had followed her advice. That project required a high level of technology and was not easy to manage, given the subpar capabilities of the KIS team. He had come to put the KIS team's technical abilities to the test. This client was a Ph.D. in wireless and mathematics. He had a commanding voice and a dark complexion. He was born in South Africa but moved to California for his Ph.D. there. The way he was talking, it appeared that the KIS team had no chance, at all. A meeting and technical discussion were scheduled to address his concerns about the domain experience and capability of the KIS team. It was an in-depth technical discussion.

He technically grilled Kavi in that meeting in a ruthless manner. Kavi was under intense pressure to stand firm, but he couldn't, and his so-called followers were also hiding their faces in the face of Atkin's probing questions. Kavi, being the astute individual he was, gradually began to pass on all questions to Sarvesh. Sarvesh, with his experience and in-depth genuine technical capability, could nicely answer Atkin's questions, backed up by factual data. He remained calm and composed while responding. Atkin was paying close attention to Sarvesh's confidence and responses. He was the only guy in that meeting who could answer satisfactorily because he also understood the system level and academic aspects of the work. That day was a one-man show, and it appeared that only two people were talking during the two-hour meeting, Sarvesh and Atkin. Atkin's bouncers were on one end, and Sarvesh's responses were like the classic batting, by a veteran cricketer.

Finally, Atkin was very impressed and desired a short break. During the break, in the corridor, he privately and fondly asked him, "Sarvesh, I am delighted to meet people like you." But, how many Engineers like you are there in KIS? Please let me know the truth. I do not think that you have acquired all this knowledge in KIS, right? Where did you work before?" Sarvesh was stumped for an immediate response. After that meeting, it appeared that Atkin had a good idea that there weren't many people on the same level as Sarvesh. To keep KIS's respect, he had to tell a half-truth and told him that there were 3 to 4 more people like him. "Really?" Atkin inquired. "I don't believe so." That's where the conversation ended. Following the meeting, Atkin expressed satisfaction and requested that the KIS team submit a techno-commercial proposal response. At this point, Kavi showed little interest because he was personally afraid of Atkin and worried that Sarvesh would shine in that project. If the KIS management had asked Sarvesh, he would have suggested starting the project with a positive attitude. Any gaps in resource capability could always be filled by hiring people laterally whom Sarvesh could have mentored. But it was clear that Kavi did not want this project because he felt insulted. After all, he couldn't answer any of Atkin's questions properly! Kavi was taking the happenings personally and it was not correct. Putting personal ego ahead of organizational benefits was very immature. In any case, it was a missed opportunity for KIS.

The following year, Sarvesh travelled to the United States several times for important project work. These projects provided the KIS team with valuable technical domain experience and significant revenue benefits. He ensured that the team and the organization benefited whenever he travelled outside India or even when he performed initiatives from India. However, a small group of ineffective team members were constantly indulging in some negative gossiping about how he was attracting attention, etc. They were oblivious to his tireless efforts and personal sacrifices in this process. He continued to make some more official trips abroad, away from his family and with little monetary compensation. He was successful in obtaining numerous business and project possibilities for KIS. However, he could never take his family with him because the KIS process prevented him from covering the cost of flying and other expenses. No one from KIS management ever facilitated his family trips or even mentioned it to him, let alone paid for his travel!

One such trip to the United States for the UIDC Project is worth mentioning. He was traveling alone, with no other KIS staff accompanying him. During this trip, he was in a near-plane crash and faced a life-or-death crisis! The following is a description of the incident. Sarvesh had a layover in Frankfurt before continuing to the United States on this trip. His first flight took him from Chennai to Frankfurt, en route to Los Angeles. While flying across western Asia and the Gulf deserts, he could see the dry and hot sunlight streaming in through the plane's windows, as it was a bright day. He couldn't get a good night's sleep the night before due to a busy workload. As a result, he was exhausted and fell asleep on the plane. He awoke after a while, freshened up, and listened to some old lovely, popular songs by Bollywood legend Kishore Kumar. People were strolling down the aisle, front and rear, enjoying their afternoon munchies, and so on.

Suddenly, Sarvesh felt the plane plummet vertically by a significant distance, and people around him began to rush to their seats. Everyone started to scream in a horrifying tone. The flight attendants hurried to their seats, announcing that something horrible had occurred and attempting to calm people down. However, they had no control over the situation. The upper luggage cabins automatically opened, and some of the luggage items dropped and struck some passengers, seriously injuring them. Some folks also went back and forth in the aisle, uncontrollably sliding from front to rear. They were the guys who hadn't taken their seats and were standing near the restrooms. These vertical dives lasted over 20 to 30 minutes, which was not a typical turbulence. Sarvesh was praying to all his Hindu Gods and Goddesses at the time of the tragedy. He prayed to God to keep him alive so he might see his wife, children, and parents when he returned home.

"If I had done anything good in life, this jet would be safe again," he had genuinely prayed and pleaded to God. The moment he uttered these words silently, he could feel the jet was slowly getting back on track. He felt relieved and noted that many individuals had suddenly started ordering alcoholic beverages, which they quickly consumed before falling asleep. Perhaps they were so horrified by the situation that they didn't want to be awake and turned to booze to forget about it. Later, he learned that a high-flying eagle or other bird had struck the plane's fan blades, and it was only by God's grace that the aircraft was still flying and all passengers were still alive. Even though the German pilots had a lot of flying experience and solid expertise, they were also taken aback by the occurrence. Sarvesh, on the other hand, would never forget that event. Later, every time he flew, he was reminded of how fragile and valuable human life is. When he arrived in the United States, he told his wife about it, and she was really speechless and yet relieved, thanking God that he was still alive.

To only highlight Sarvesh's project-related contributions would be insufficient. During his time at KIS-UIDC, he accomplished much more. When he was in the Chennai office and working on projects in India, he was also involved in other aspects, such as industry-academic partnerships. He was looking after additional commitments for the overall branding of the team and the company. Both academia and organization benefited from this collaboration. Sarvesh used to extract time from his personal commitments on weekends and late at night. In one such program, a trip to Coimbatore was arranged for him to give a one-week training program at VCE College of Engineering. Along with him was another KIS colleague who was supposed to join him to cover the training aspects of his domain. However, he did not join at the last minute, and Sarvesh ended up training and covering his portion for the students at VCE. This time, he booked tickets for his wife and children to accompany him. He planned to take his family to nearby places of attractions in his spare time. It was a local trip within the state to another city that required an overnight train ride from Chennai. The company did not pay for the tickets that they could have purchased if they so desired. Anyway, the next day, he and his family got off the train and went to the college guest house, where a room was reserved for him and his family.

During his stay, he was extremely busy at college and had little time to explore the city and its environs. His family was bored because they were only staying at the guest house. One day, when he was in college during that stay, he received a call from the guest house informing him that his wife and children had been injured by falling and severely injuring themselves. His younger child's head was smacked against the edge of the bed. His wife had slipped on the floor because the room was crammed with old furniture and the floor was slippery. It had harmed both her and the child. In that sense, it was a bad trip, and he felt guilty for not declining the trip, which affected his family. He was also wondering why he had accepted the extra burden from the other KIS colleague! Regardless, thanks to God's grace, on the last day of their stay in Coimbatore, he was able to carve out some time to visit a nearby famous temple! They offered prayers, which he recalls vividly as a somewhat consoling experience. In addition, they rushed through the city and a nearby small old fort in a couple of hours, leaving no time for shopping. However, one of the college students presented them with the famous silk sari. He thanked him for his kind gesture. His children were somewhat scared in that fort, which was in shabby due to construction at the time. Sarvesh was a good storyteller who told his children some terrifying tales about the fort. He described how the Manjulika (or Chandramukhi) ghost character from movies was pictured in that location. That marked the end of the journey. The next day, they returned to Chennai, and he resumed his routine work at the office.

It was 2008, and the projects at KIS-UIDC were ongoing at a normal pace, but a few engineers were not getting enough work, and the client did not have a long-term vision for them. As a result, the KIS team desired to detach them from UIDC and use them in another client's project to generate significantly more revenue.

However, those engineers were not technically equipped to be deployed as per the requirements of the new project. As a result, Kavi asked Sarvesh to mentor them at the time. "Sarvesh, you are a great individual performer, but I want you to excel further in your career, so I want you to train these two engineers (Venu and Nepak) and prepare them for other projects," he said. You should share your knowledge with others so that the team members do not think of you as only an individual contributor. I want to challenge you to change people's perceptions about you!" Sarvesh had no idea that Kavi was plotting a clever scheme to get his work done while advancing his own career through Sarvesh's efforts.

The statement that Sarvesh did not share his knowledge with others was completely false and intended to insult him. Sarvesh, on the other hand, did not argue and silently accepted his challenge. He wanted to prove everyone wrong. Sarvesh's acceptance of the challenge to guide these two senior engineers was already a winning point for Kavi. Following that, the journey was a completely different and challenging experience for Sarvesh, who had to do his regular work for the UIDC client for nearly 8 to 9 hours while also mentoring, guiding, and hand-holding these two engineers for the new project. Sarvesh, by the way, recently won this project entirely on his own. For this project, KIS management had sent him to the United States for two weeks to convince the client technically. The client team was highly experienced, and they had asked him some difficult questions to which he could convincingly respond. KIS had initially told him that he would only be involved in that project for a few weeks. But, gradually, he realized that his involvement was in increasing order, and the scope was expanding. Following another discussion with Kavi, it was clear that the KIS higher management desired Sarvesh to devote additional time and effort beyond his UIDC work! This was unexpected. As a result, his daily workload nearly doubled. This meant that he would have to arrive at the office early and leave even later, almost every day for the next 8 to 9 months. Many nights, he had missed the local transportation schedule. He used to walk for kilometres in the middle of the night to get home, and he did so many times during the rainy season, putting his life in danger. His conviction and hope were to prove himself to Kavi and others wrong.

In the months that followed, he had no idea when his children went to bed or when they went to school! He also missed the holidays and weekends. Throughout those many months until the end of that project, Kavi never bothered to ask how this new project was progressing and whether any support was needed. He was sure that with Sarvesh on board, no project could afford to fail. During those many months, Sarvesh did not and could not take any leave. Whenever he had a break from UIDC, the new project exploited his free time regularly. He continued to observe his colleagues enjoying their life and free time at the cafeteria or an indoor game. He proposed many new innovative ideas to the customer during this project, and they were delighted and appreciated him and the two engineers got immensely benefited from this. This team of Sarvesh and two engineers could create a fantastic prototype product in a short period. He had thoroughly mentored these two engineers and brought them up to the level that Kavi and the client expected. The client's prototype product was showcased in one of the popular International Exhibitions in the United States and received an award in the innovative category. It also captured the interest of the end-users. Finally, this project was a huge success for the KIS team and generated a lot of revenue. It also proved to be an excellent learning platform for Venu and Nepak, who were mentored by Sarvesh and eventually became self-sufficient after working on this project under his supervision. Later, with these two people, KIS benefited greatly in many project executions, even after Sarvesh left the KIS organization.

Around the middle of 2008-09, a pattern of reduced project inflow and slower revenue generation was observed in KIS and many other similar organizations. This was the period preceding the global financial recession. Sarvesh was still a part of UIDC, and while the number of projects had decreased, he was still overburdened with work. KIS management was already considering consolidating the knowledge base amassed thus far through UIDC engagement. During one Friday afternoon snack time, Kavi invited Sarvesh to a conference room and asked him how to compile these technical details into a document format. Sarvesh pondered over it the following weekend and came up with the brilliant idea of compiling all of the contents into a handbook. His concept was that the technical essence should be covered while preventing the leakage of any customer copyrighted or proprietary materials. Based on his concept, he created a rough draft of the entire book. Also, he created a more extensive scope for all team members to contribute at least one to two technical papers each. He presented that concept to Kavi. Kavi became a little excited about this. At the same time, Sarvesh sensed that Kavi was envious of the idea of such a book concept. He wanted this book to be finished, but he didn't want Sarvesh to take credit for it! Anyway, he appeared interested in this idea, so he gave Sarvesh permission to proceed.

Sarvesh's next major task was to teach every team member how to write technical papers. They had never done such high-quality work before in their careers. As a result, they were skeptical at first. Their confidence was shaky, which he could sense. Furthermore, some guys were envious of this idea and did not want Sarvesh to shine in this activity. They were always busy finding the negative aspects of whatever he did and so opposed this frequently and made this work appear to be a failure. However, he continued to engage and motivate the team's like-minded engineers, and they began to contribute to this book. He taught them how to write papers systematically. It took nearly three months to complete that book, and several reviews and corrections were also performed. Sarvesh was not only an individual contributor to some of his papers but also the book's chief editor. After all, it was his idea, and his goal was to take this type of handbook to the global stage and make this team's presence known. He could have written such a book on his own. On the other hand, he preferred to share his knowledge with everyone. This noble effort of his was a huge success. However, due to Kavi's indifferent attitude, this book remained within the team's boundaries alone. Kavi took the completed book to his boss and projected it as if he had only coordinated and done that great work. Sarvesh was unaware of this until the final days of his stay at KIS. This book was highly beneficial to Kavi. He was promoted, and thanks to Sarvesh's efforts, he could extract the team's vast knowledge base effectively. Kavi also used that book for his knowledge-gathering whenever he needed to learn something because he lacked domain expertise. This book was a 400-page solid knowledge database for the KIS team to refer to and benefit from, in the coming years.

Finally, it was nearing the end of 2008 when the KIS-UIDC had no significant projects because it was the time of the great global financial market collapse and a severe slowdown in all industries. As a result, KIS and UWT were no exception and were not immune to it. People were losing their jobs all over the place. As a result, the UIDC engagement was almost closed down, and the KIS management took advantage of the opportunity to use Sarvesh's knowledge for whatever they desired. He was still a billed resource in the UIDC, and the client had requested that he be relocated to their Mumbai office. But, Kavi played another dirty trick, detaching Sarvesh from a billable UIDC project. Sarvesh was assigned to a different domain project so that, with his technical leadership, many other team members could be saved during this downtime. Kavi was essentially fighting for his own and his followers' survival. If Sarvesh had left KIS at that time, the team would have crumbled, and everyone would have lost their jobs. Anyway, Sarvesh was trapped again, and because everything had happened without his knowledge, he was completely unaware of this. He thus accepted this challenge because he did not want to leave Chennai abruptly.

By this time, the KIS team had asked the entire team to re-skill for a different domain for this new project within a couple of months. Sarvesh was asked to lead this other domain project and was given the difficult task of training others in that new domain in a short time while also executing the project in real-time. In this scenario, he taught himself and the entire team in non-domain and completed the project from the ground up. During that time, he and a small group of team members slogged for days and nights learning new things and getting up to speed in a brief period, which was never easy. In that phase, some team members who were closer to Kavi, had cleverly avoided doing the actual work. This project was also a massive success after six months of hard work and dedication. Sarvesh would frequently arrive home around 3 or 4 a.m. during this project. No one in higher management truly appreciated his efforts because Kavi and his followers systematically stole all the credit.

This was the time for the yearly appraisal for that year, and Sarvesh was naturally expecting to be acknowledged and rewarded for all of his hard work and excellent holistic contributions. However, when the appraisal results were released, he discovered that he received only a meagre pay raise and there was no career promotion for him. Kavi tried hard to console him that the team's performance had suffered due to the global slowdown! Sarvesh, on the other hand, learned that two people had been promoted to the next level with a higher salary. It meant that one of them had risen above Sarvesh's level and grade as a result of the team manager, Kavi's, great favor to these guys. Also, Kavi himself had been promoted to the General Manager level. Sarvesh realized at that point that the manager had revealed his true colors. But he couldn't believe how the higher management team didn't recognize his contributions. He felt side-lined entirely and all his good work had been hijacked. He felt terrible for his family because they had to make so many sacrifices for him, and he appeared to be working for some crooks in the organizations. This was the pinnacle of his exploitation. The manager's and his superiors' hypocrisy was obviously visible by now.

Sarvesh was devastated and decided to take a few days off to look for a new job. Suddenly, one of his college batch mates called him around that time, and during that brief conversation, he asked him if he had any positions available in his company. The job was in Sarvesh's hometown, which was thousands of miles away from Chennai. It was the middle of the school year for his children, who were enrolled in a school in Chennai. As a result, the decision to relocate was difficult for him and his family. He decided to go first, and the family would follow after the academic year. So he was being separated from his family due to this vile manager and his terrible actions. He resigned from his job one day and was so depressed that he wanted to return to his hometown. Things happened so quickly for him that he was following his instincts and couldn't feel respected enough to stay in KIS, even if management wanted him to reconsider his decisions. Subsequently, the manager, Kavi expressed regret over his appraisal decisions and privately admitted to Sarvesh that he had made a grave error. In any case, Sarvesh had already decided, and he was a man of words. He had already accepted the new job offer from his friend's company and always kept his word.

During this time, Kavi also attempted to offer Sarvesh some solace about future career opportunities at KIS. Sarvesh, on the other hand, was not convinced because he had utterly lost faith in this manager by that point. He believed that leaving KIS was a significant turning point in his career, and he is unsure whether it was for the better or worse. But as a result, his own family had suffered greatly, and he was filled with remorse. He wanted to escape to his native place with the new job offer in hand because he was already feeling choked in his career, the metro cities, and the hypocritical people around him. He was thinking about the root cause of his career upheaval at the time was the Indian manager, Kavi.

After hearing this explanation, Mr. Andy, the Whizwin Corp's interview panelist, was wholly immersed in the thought of Sarvesh's journey. He needed some time to accept the reality of the situation. He had almost forgotten that he was taking an interview until that point and instead told Sarvesh that it was like a web series of eventful moments and a lot of learning in life insights he had gained from these interactions. "Don't worry, Mr. Sarvesh," he assured him. “You will be working with a global team and will not have to make such sacrifices in your personal life. We, as a company, do not ask our employees to sacrifice their personal lives for the sake of the job." He was pleased with Sarvesh's handling of company matters and everything else. He told Sarvesh, smiling, that the next round of interviews would be held soon and that he should be prepared.

Following that day's discussion, the HR person called Sarvesh to inform him that Andy's interview feedback was very positive and that the following interview would be held in the subsequent week. The HR representative wished him good luck in the next round and a happy weekend. Sarvesh reciprocated by wishing the same. That night, he wondered if he should have accepted Kavi's offer to stay back at KIS many years ago. He wondered if his life would have been different if he hadn't reacted so quickly to Kavi's blunder. He was pondering over the proverb, "An eye for an eye makes the whole world blind!" Sarvesh would most likely have settled in the United States, as Kavi had recently offered to send him there the following year. However, he also wondered if people like Kavi would ever keep his words in real life! Anyway, it had been a destiny journey for Sarvesh. When all the wheels of the life vehicle are well-balanced, only then the rider arrives at his destination smoothly and enjoys a wholesome life journey. Unfortunately, this was not the case with Sarvesh thus far.

About the Authors

The Couple-Authors (Usha, Saroj) are budding authors who are here to make some positive changes in society through their thought-provoking storytelling technique.

Ms Usharani Panda (MBA-Finance, MA-English, B.Ed.-Distinction & University Topper) is an experienced and dedicated teacher, principal, and mentor to many students in her academic journey. She is highly qualified in her field of teaching. She specializes in Indian and Global literature. She had also worked briefly in a corporate career before moving to the academic field. She is an observing individual who welcomes life as it comes and retains the positives and filters out the negatives. As per her hope, one day this world shall be a wonderful place for all to live in with harmony and without greed, fear, jealousy, etc. She is a believer and a seeker in life. She is logical and traditional both at the same time. She has her own Youtube Channel (i.e., USHA THE QUEEN VLOGGER) through which she spreads happiness and Indian value systems, and traditional and modern food preparation methods. Her style of explanation is very much simple and yet unique.

Dr Saroj K. Patro (PhD in Electronics and Communications Engineering) is a highly experienced corporate professional who has worked at many organisations and has been a pillar of many technological developments throughout his organisational career. He has a great interest in

Technology, Music, Literature, Human Values, Ethical Friendship, Selfless Mentoring, etc. He believes that technology and humanity should co-exist always as mutually benefitting entities. He is a person who values Indian traditional value systems. His concern is about the rapidly deteriorating state of Indian good old traditions due to the greed and worldly desires of some bunch of people in the modern-day. He is positive that one day, Grandma's good-old-days story-type surroundings shall prevail again in real life where everyone will be a happy person, irrespective of their age, religion, caste, gender, colour, etc. without any human-created boundaries.

Keep Connected

Instagram
Usha: https://www.instagram.com/ushapanda80/
Saroj:
https://www.instagram.com/sarojpatroindianmusicals/

Facebook
Usha: https://www.facebook.com/usha.panda.58/
Saroj: https://www.facebook.com/saroj.patro.98

Youtube
Usha:
https://www.youtube.com/c/USHATHEQUEENVLOGGER

LinkedIn
Usha:-https://www.linkedin.com/in/usha-saroj-p-1b9936246/